Alexander Mack:

A Man Who Rippled the Waters

Written by Myrna Grove

Illustrated by Mary Jewell

Dedication

For my parents, Kedric and Florence Grove,
whose lives exemplified the spirit of Christian service and love
—*Myrna*

For Jeanne and my children and family,
encouraging them to plant seeds and keep their dreams alive.
—*Mary*

Cover: The year 2008 marks the 300th anniversary of the first baptisms among the German Baptists in the Eder River of Schwarzenau, Germany, in 1708. Inspired by Alexander Mack, the group included Alexander and Anna Mack, Andrew and Joanna Boni, George Grebe, John and Johanna Kipping, and Lucas Vetter. The baptisms marked the beginning of the Brethren movement.

Acknowledgments

We appreciate the following who encouraged and supported the *Alexander Mack* book project: Jeanne Jacoby Smith, Professor of English at McPherson College; Dale Ulrich, former Professor and Dean of Bridgewater College; Myrna Flory (Bob) Gemmer, Ecumenical Workers with National and World Councils of Churches; Hans Joerg Schmidt, Archivist in Schriesheim, Germany; Otto Marburger, Historian in Schwarzenau, Germany; and Roger Jewell, Author and Historian.

Printed in the United States of America

Library of Congress Number: 2008924446
International Standard Book Number: 978-1-60126-103-8

Alexander Mack: A Man Who Rippled the Waters/Myrna Grove. 1st ed.
The illustrations were done on clayboard in oils using transparent layers.
Fragments from European artists of the period were also incorporated.

Summary: Tells about the life of religious leader, Alexander Mack in 18th century Germany. Mack was the organizer and first minister of the Brethren movement. In 1729, he migrated to Germantown, Pennsylvania, where the church expanded.

1. Mack, Alexander, 1679-1735 – Biography – Juvenile Literature.
2. Germany - Biography – Juvenile Literature
3. Church of the Brethren – History – Juvenile Literature

I. Jewell, Mary, ill. II. Title.

286.5 dc22

Printed by
Masthof Press
219 Mill Road
Morgantown, PA 19543-9516
www.masthof.com

Table of Contents

Early Life 1679—1706

Young Alexander Mack carefully steered his small wooden cart through the narrow streets of Schriesheim. Following his father's strict orders, Alexander was taking bags of flour to nearby neighbors. His three older brothers could be trusted to drive wagonloads of flour to farmers near the river. But Alexander must first prove himself by making deliveries to the tile-roofed houses down the street.

Alexander knew that his father would hear from customers if he made a mistake. Alexander was a little envious that his sisters got to stay home and help their mother. He wished that running the mill did not take so much time. His older brothers seemed more satisfied with the work at the mill than he did. Alexander dutifully finished his tasks before sunset so he could report home.

Alexander, who was named after his mother's brother, was the eighth child born to John and Christina Mack. Shortly before Alexander's birth in 1679, his father collected money to buy back the family mill. Grandfather George Mack had lost ownership of the mill during a long period of war in Germany.

The large mill, built by Alexander's great-great-grandfather, stood beside a whole row of mills next to a small creek. Inside the Mack mill, there was a room for grinding grain, a stable for horses, and the family living quarters. Behind the mill, the Macks kept a large garden and vineyards of grapes. Young Alexander also helped his family by weeding the garden and feeding oats to the horses.

When the Mack brothers were not working, they attended school in the balcony of the church. The schoolmaster taught lessons in reading, arithmetic and writing to the young men of the village. Alexander liked to study and discuss new ideas. He hoped someday to go to the university in Heidelberg. Maybe then, his brother, George Conrad, would stop teasing him about his love for knowledge. When he went to the university, Alexander hoped to leave the work at the mill to his older brothers.

Alexander often sat eagerly on the knee of his grandfather, George Mack. Grandfather Mack shared many stories about his early days. He said that terrible armies had passed through their valley. They burned much of the village and surrounding fields.

Grandfather Mack said that, several times, the armies had damaged their timber-framed homes and the church tower. One time, soldiers even set fire to the Mack mill. To save the town hall bells, villagers secretly lowered them down a deep well. Then, soldiers could not use the metal to make more cannons.

"The battles of one war lasted so long," stated Grandfather Mack to wide-eyed Alexander, "that it became known as the Thirty Years War! The people of Schriesheim suffered greatly when soldiers ruined our crops and killed animals for food. At times, our family hid in the mountains where we gathered wild berries and roots to eat."

Germany was split into three hundred provinces. Whenever a new prince conquered a tiny German state, he would change the laws to suit himself. When the fighting ended, villagers would return from camping in the forest. They rebuilt their homes, planted new crops and repaired the church. Grandfather Mack was installed as mayor of Schriesheim. And, for a short period of time, the valley remained at peace.

The Reformed Church in Schriesheim had the most members. The Mack family regularly attended its services, and John Mack was a respected elder. It was the custom to baptize all newborn babies in the church. Pastor Ludwig Agricola had baptized all eleven children born to John and Christina Mack, including Alexander.

When Alexander was just nine years old, he was saddened by the death of his grandfather. George Mack had served as Schriesheim's mayor for three decades, longer than anyone else. He had guided the villagers through many troubling events. As his coffin was carried through the winding streets to the burial ground, townspeople mourned their loss. Alexander followed closely behind and thought to himself, "I will never forget grandfather's heartbreaking stories."

Soon afterwards, Alexander's oldest brother died. Now, Alexander was forced to give up his dream of going to the university. His family would need him at home.

At the age of twelve, Alexander and his friends prepared for their confirmation in the Reformed Church. They studied the strict ideas of church leaders such as John Calvin. Alexander began to read verses in the Bible and wonder how Jesus wanted his followers to live.

Before long, an army from France marched through the valley. French soldiers badly burned the city and the castle of nearby Heidelberg. Villagers in the area again ran to the dark, forested hills for safety.

During this unsettled time, the villagers appointed Alexander's father as town mayor. Alexander wanted his father to stop the fighting. As mayor, John Mack sent gifts and money to the French army. By doing this, he hoped they would not destroy the village.

When the French army left, German soldiers quickly moved in. Not only was the village running out of money, but now, there were no crops to harvest. Older boys in the village were forced to become soldiers. Alexander watched the horror of war up close. He experienced hunger and terror much like his Grandfather Mack had once described.

Alexander and his family fled back to the forests. They built a rough shelter of branches and sod in which to hide. While huddled inside with his family, Alexander thought about what Jesus would say to the warring soldiers in the valley below.

When he was finally able to return home, Alexander felt restless and uneasy. "My heart is not in the work at the mill," he told his father.

One person who listened closely to Alexander's doubts and dreams was Anna Margaret Kling. Alexander had known Anna since childhood, but now he thought of her in a special way. The two of them sat on the hillside for hours as they talked about their hopes for the future.

As their love for each other grew stronger, Alexander and Anna decided to marry. They were wed in Schriesheim's village church by the same pastor who had baptized them as babies. Because Anna's father served on the town council and her grandfather had been Heidelberg's mayor, many important persons came to the wedding.

After their marriage, Anna moved in with her husband's family at the Mack mill. Nearly a year later, Alexander and Anna were blessed with their first child, a son. Alexander's mother joyfully welcomed her first grandchild. The entire Mack family was present for the baby's baptism at the Reformed Church.

The next year, Alexander's mother unexpectedly died. His father, John Mack, greatly missed the love and support of his dear wife, Christina. Without her, he decided that the mill and household were too much work for him. He divided the mill property equally between his sons, Jacob and Alexander. To his son, George Conrad, who was a baker in Ladenburg, he gave a house.

Soon, a war broke out between Germany and Spain. Once again, soldiers invited themselves into the homes of villagers and ate food from their tables. Villagers paid heavy taxes, and the Macks provided flour from their mill to passing armies. Alexander became discouraged as he obeyed these rules of war. One bright event which softened his heart during this time was the birth of a second son.

Because wars near Schriesheim never seemed to end, Alexander felt helpless. By now, all but three of Alexander's brothers and sisters had died. Why does God allow such suffering? he wondered. The pastor at the village church seemed to take more interest in money and power than in answering Alexander's questions.

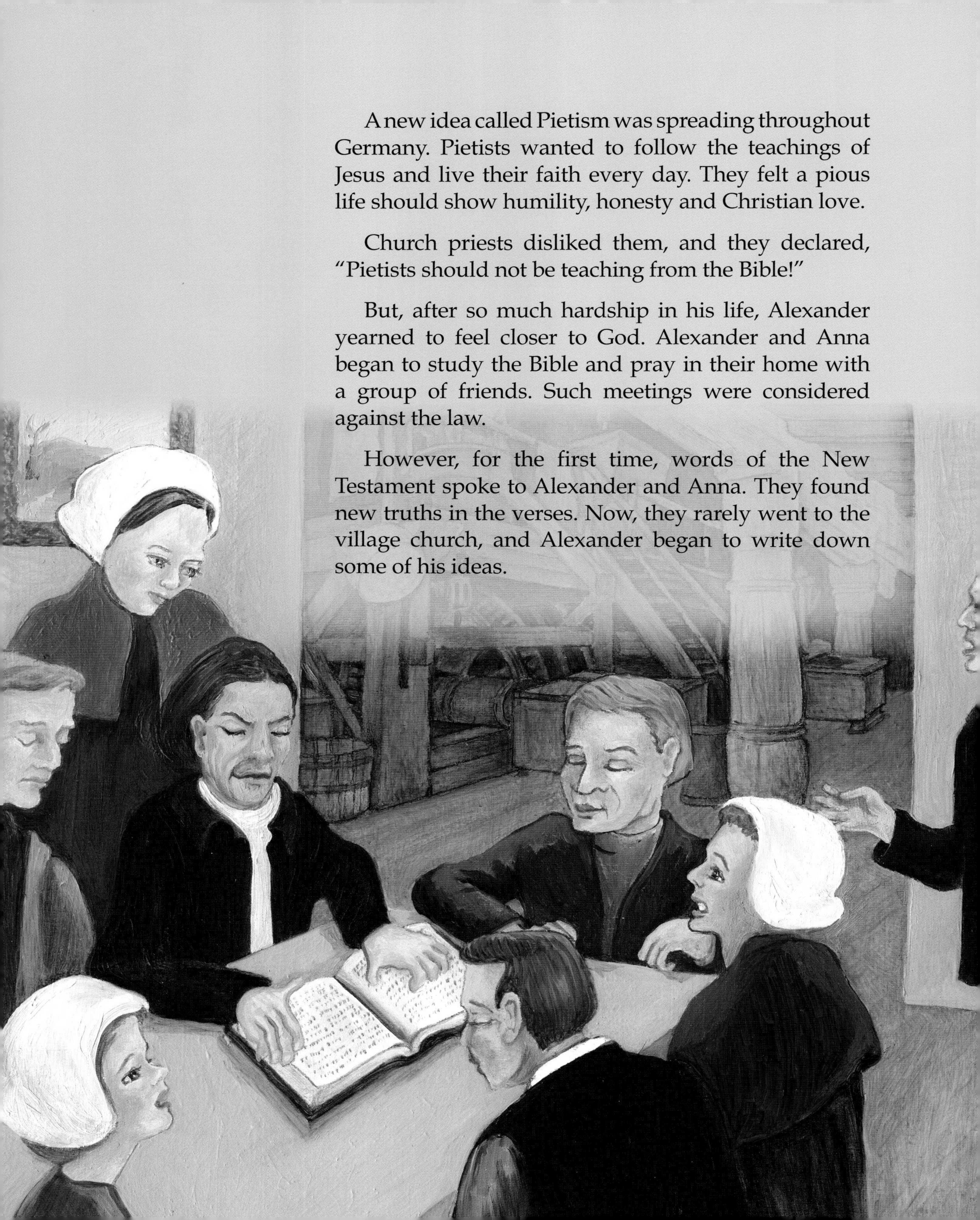

A new idea called Pietism was spreading throughout Germany. Pietists wanted to follow the teachings of Jesus and live their faith every day. They felt a pious life should show humility, honesty and Christian love.

Church priests disliked them, and they declared, "Pietists should not be teaching from the Bible!"

But, after so much hardship in his life, Alexander yearned to feel closer to God. Alexander and Anna began to study the Bible and pray in their home with a group of friends. Such meetings were considered against the law.

However, for the first time, words of the New Testament spoke to Alexander and Anna. They found new truths in the verses. Now, they rarely went to the village church, and Alexander began to write down some of his ideas.

Some farmers who came to the Mack mill were called Mennonites. The Mennonites had fled to Germany from Switzerland. Their name came from Menno Simons, a Dutch priest who united them in their beliefs. They had settled in the ravaged land of southern Germany after the Thirty Years War.

In Switzerland, Mennonites had been punished for ignoring the laws of the church. They had refused to become soldiers. And, they were imprisoned for not baptizing their children. Because they believed in baptizing adults, they were known as rebaptizers, or Anabaptists.

Alexander thought the Mennonites were peaceful and honest. He admired many of their beliefs. They were skilled farmers, and Alexander did what he could at his mill to assist them. Sometimes, he discussed his ideas about the church with them.

Each month, Alexander delivered flour to the nearby town of Mannheim. While there one month in 1704, he heard a powerful preacher named Ernst Christoph Hochmann. Hochmann spent most of his time traveling the Rhine River Valley telling people about the love of Jesus. Because of his free spirit toward religious beliefs, Hochmann was often imprisoned in castle dungeons by the authorities.

Eventually, Alexander sold half of the mill to his brother, Jacob. At the mill, Alexander still reserved use of the great room and kitchen for Pietist meetings. His ideas against the church caused his father, John Mack, much heartache. Shortly after Alexander quit helping at the mill, his father died.

Meanwhile, Hochmann traveled in the German states preaching and teaching. Hochmann openly preached God's message to farmers and villagers on the streets. This angered and frightened Reformed Church leaders.

Alexander invited Hochmann to his mill, hoping villagers would be inspired to renew their faith. Hochmann's preaching went so well that more than fifty persons joined the Pietists. The church council in Heidelberg became alarmed. They sent an officer to find out if the Pietists were following church laws. The officer threatened to arrest them if they were not.

To avoid arrest, Alexander Mack, his wife, and two sons gathered a few possessions and quietly escaped into the woods Alexander knew so well. They followed a hilly path south for ten kilometers. In the city of Heidelberg, the Macks were taken in by some kind Mennonites. However, Pietists were not treated much better there. Officers threw rocks at homes where Pietists met. They were not safe in one place for very long.

Hochmann returned to Mannheim where he was soon arrested. Alexander visited him in prison. But, officers asked Alexander to leave town. Later, state officials wrote a decree that all Pietists should be arrested. As a warning to them, Hochmann was sent away without a trial to build walls along the Neckar River.

But wherever Hochmann was working, a crowd would gather. Men of many ranks traveled far to hear him preach. Hochmann gained even more attention when soldiers beat him. When he promised never to return to southern Germany, Hochmann was finally set free.

The Move to Schwarzenau 1706

During this time of upheaval, the Mack family stayed out of sight. Alexander still wrote down his ideas and shared them with other Pietists. Even though Alexander did not seek to be a leader, others began to follow him. Alexander's patience and sincerity, along with his skills for organizing, helped spread his influence.

To keep his family from harm, Alexander moved them north in 1706 to the town of Schwarzenau. In the peace of the Eder River Valley, the Macks found a loving group of neighbors. The ruler of the province, Count Henry Albert, welcomed them and accepted their differences.

In Schwarzenau, the gentle slopes had not been overrun by soldiers. Dense forests protected the small town and provided a living for the villagers. A large manor house stood in the center of town beside an arching stone bridge. Farmers lived in a row of small houses close to the meandering river.

So many Pietists arrived in town that they built simple huts on a wooded hillside. These crude cabins above Schwarzenau became known as the Valley of Huts. The Mack family bought a more substantial house, and Alexander invited other persons who had separated from the church to come to his home.

On Sunday afternoons and some evenings, families and individuals met around the Mack fireplace. They sang hymns and prayed. In the dim light, Alexander read from the Bible, and the group searched for guidance in the scriptures. When Hochmann was able to come, he interpreted the words for them.

To provide money for his family, Alexander sometimes worked at the town mill. But, mostly, Alexander traveled to villages in the area to preach. At times, his friend, Hochmann, joined him. They went as far south as the slopes of Switzerland.

Pietists in Schwarzenau believed in helping one another. They shared needed supplies and shelter. Since Alexander had inherited money, he gave food and aid to the others. He especially cared for the needs of new church members.

Alexander and Anna wrote letters back to their family in Schriesheim. Because Anna's father and mother supported the Pietists, they were asked to leave the Reformed Church. They also paid a heavy fine and were confined, for a time, in a dungeon.

Families in Schwarzenau were still concerned about baptism. Baptizing adults was a crime punishable by death. Alexander searched the Bible, but he couldn't find a verse about the baptism of infants. Most Pietists felt called to a new life by the Holy Spirit. Some wanted to be baptized in a river like Jesus. Hochmann warned them that they should carefully consider the consequences of such a forbidden act.

Early on an August morning in 1708, after much prayer and reflection, eight persons followed their hearts' desires. Just as the sun rose through the mist, Alexander Mack led the small, shivering group toward the arching stone bridge in the center of Schwarzenau. Five men and three women gathered on the banks of the Eder River. Anna Mack stood loyally beside her husband. The men cast lots to see who would baptize Alexander.

After they had sung several hymns and read scripture from Luke 14 about counting the cost, Alexander waded into the cool water. Kneeling, he answered the vows of baptism. As he bent forward, his head was dipped into the water three times "in the name of the Father, and of the Son, and of the Holy Spirit." After his baptism, Alexander stood up in the water and, in turn, baptized and prayed for each of the others.

Count Well the Cost

Christ Jesus says, "Count well the cost
When you lay the foundation."
Are you resolved, though all seem lost,
To risk your reputation,
Your self, your wealth, for Christ the Lord
As you now give your solemn word?

Into Christ's death you're buried now
Through baptism's joyous union.
No claim of self dare you allow
If you desire communion
With Christ's true church, His willing bride,
Which, through His Word, He has supplied.

Word of the baptisms spread quickly to other villages. Alexander Mack was now the recognized leader of the group. The New Baptists believed they could speak directly to God. Everyone could receive the gift of Jesus and show His love to others.

By their actions, the small group was now known as New Baptists. It had not been their plan, but they had started a new church body of believers. Some of the other Pietists did not approve of the baptisms. Hadn't they disobeyed the law? What would happen to them now?

For communion, the New Baptists met in a large room of the Mack home. They set up two tables, one for men and one for women. First, they spent time praising God. Then, they listened to the Bible story about Jesus washing the feet of his disciples. Only those members who felt prepared would stay to participate.

As Jesus told his disciples to do, each one knelt to wash the feet of the person beside him. They ate a simple meal of bread and beef broth. After Alexander blessed the communion bread and the wine, each one passed bread to his neighbor and drank from a common cup.

The New Baptists began to develop their beliefs. At first, they decided to share all their possessions. Because they often traveled to share their ideas, they did not hold regular jobs. They paid their taxes, but they did not believe in taking oaths.

For a short time, the New Baptists did not live in separate family groups. Though some were already married, they wanted to devote all their time to serving God. However, this practice did not last, and four years later, Alexander and Anna had another son. They named him Alexander Mack, Jr. Soon, they had two daughters, but sadly, the youngest one died as a baby.

To keep members faithful, the New Baptists practiced the ban. If one of them sinned, he was expected to ask for forgiveness. If he refused, he could not participate in worship services, and no one was allowed to speak with him.

It is not surprising that the New Baptists were against war. Many times in their lives, they had witnessed the suffering of war. They did not believe that fighting was the way to carry out God's plans.

Soon after the Eder River baptisms, Hochmann cut his ties with the New Baptists. He especially disagreed with their outward practices of disciplining church members. For several years, Hochmann had inspired them as a leader, and Alexander had loved him like a brother. Alexander was disturbed that his dear friend now spoke out against New Baptist beliefs.

In 1710, the brother-in-law of Count Henry Albert made a list of charges against the New Baptists whom he called fanatics. He did not approve of their private meetings where both men and women spoke. He didn't like their refusal to baptize infants, yet rebaptize adults. He also disliked the New Baptist practices of communion and their lack of regard for social ranks and positions. However, Count Henry Albert replied that their quiet lives did not offend him as long as they obeyed civil laws and paid their taxes.

In just a few years, church membership grew from the original eight persons to two hundred. New church groups were started in three nearby towns. Alexander continued to baptize new members in the Eder River. He held worship services outdoors at a spot called the Täufergarten, or Baptist Garden. The New Baptists lived simply and quietly. Count Henry Albert still defended them and invited their leaders to his manor house.

Alexander also devoted time to writing the work called *Rights and Ordinances of the House of God*. He penned his writings in the form of conversations between a father and his son. His writings covered topics such as baptism, communion, oaths, scriptures, marriage and rewards for the faithful. Alexander hoped that his writings would explain New Baptist beliefs to other groups who were moving to Schwarzenau.

A new congregation was started in the Marienborn area. When members there became threatened because of their Pietist activities, they moved to Krefeld. Peter Becker was among the leaders in Krefeld. By 1719, a group of twenty families in Krefeld decided to leave Germany and move to the colony of Pennsylvania. Known as German Baptists, they were even experiencing disagreements with each other. Some of them did not want a separate church. Others argued about whether or not members should marry outsiders.

An Englishman named William Penn promised them inexpensive land if they would settle in Pennsylvania. Penn also promised them freedom to worship as they wanted. By moving to America, the Krefeld group hoped to leave behind their poverty and strife.

Over the years, Alexander Mack sold his personal fortune to assist church members. But now, the forests nearby did not provide enough wood for their stoves. They were even blamed for hunting too many wild game. Count Henry Albert still favored the Pietists, but he was under more pressure to not help them. Count Henry's younger brother had gained more power, and he had little sympathy for differing religious practices.

By 1720, the New Baptists in Schwarzenau made the decision to leave that area. Since they couldn't afford the trip to America, they planned instead to move farther north to the country of Holland. The Macks sold their house in Schwarzenau to Christopher Sauer, a well-known Pietist in town. Anna and their four children packed their belongings for the trip.

Before leaving, Alexander baptized his second son in the Eder River. Then, he bought travel permits from Count Henry Albert for forty families, or about two hundred people. Before they left, Mack's old friend, Hochmann, came to pray with them for a safe journey. The group tearfully bid farewell to a familiar land and walked to the Rhine River where they boarded boats headed north.

Arrival in Holland 1720

Several weeks later, the group arrived at Friesland in Northwest Holland. Close to the North Sea, the land was green and swampy. Most of the men found work digging in peat bogs. Peat was used for fuel, and blocks of peat were used for building houses. Local Mennonite families helped them settle in the small village called Surhuisterveen. Mack's group soon felt at home enough to ice skate on the frozen canals.

For nineteen years, Anna Margaret Mack had provided a loving home for her family. She had willingly supported her husband's traveling and preaching. In 1720, however, Anna suddenly became sick and died. A week later, Alexander and Anna's six-year-old daughter also died. These events were almost more pain than Alexander could bear. He alone now felt responsible for meeting the needs of his people in a strange land.

Despite his sorrow, Alexander still felt God's call to serve his flock. He ably carried on by preaching at worship services and working with his sons in the peat bogs. He baptized new church members in a local pond. Although Mack was the leader of his church, he received no pay. Besides preaching, he performed weddings and funerals, and he led communion.

Alexander was pleased to keep in touch with the Krefeld German Baptists in Pennsylvania. Letters between Pennsylvania and Holland took three to six months to cross the Atlantic Ocean. The Krefeld group had settled in the already established village of Germantown near the city of Philadelphia. Most of them joined the local weaving trade while others became farmers.

In 1723, the Krefeld group officially formed the Germantown church with Peter Becker as their leader. On Christmas Day of that year, six new persons came from the Schuylkill River valley to worship at the home of Peter Becker. Then, Peter baptized the new converts in the icy waters of Wissahickon Creek.

After mission work in the fall of 1724, two new congregations were begun in Pennsylvania including Coventry and Conestoga. Conestoga elected Johann Conrad Beissel as their leader. Beissel had been a weaver's apprentice to Peter Becker, and he was drawn to the beliefs of the German Baptists.

Alexander received news from Peter Becker with great curiosity. Peter's letters stated, "The church in America is growing, and the land is producing many kinds of fruits and crops."

Reports from Pennsylvania were encouraging to the Baptists in the peat fields of Holland. Alexander's group often had to borrow money from the Dutch to keep from starving. In Holland, the number of New Baptists was not increasing.

Eventually, Peter Becker wrote to Alexander Mack to tell him that the German Baptists in Pennsylvania now needed him as their leader. To Alexander, this opportunity for a fresh start helped him and the others make a difficult decision. They, too, would travel across the Atlantic Ocean to a new land.

The Trip to America 1729

In the spring of 1729, about thirty German Baptist families in Holland sold almost everything they had. Then, they packed wooden chests with supplies to take to America. The group traveled 200 kilometers on wagons and canal boats. Alexander had arranged for their ship passage from a port in Rotterdam.

The German Baptists boarded a small, crowded ship called the Allen. Each family dragged aboard a chest, bedding and pillows. For food, they took dried fruits, ham and brandy. Each family spread their bedding on a small space below deck as they prepared for the uncomfortable voyage.

The ship docked next in England to take on more passengers. By late June, the tiny ship set sail west across the vast ocean. From the deck, Alexander and his three sons looked back at the coastline. Alexander blinked back tears as he thought about his beloved wife, Anna. She would only make the trip with him in his heart.

Summer storms sometimes blew the ship off course. Foul water, rats and sickness caused problems on board. The trip lasted ten long weeks. When land was spotted along the Delaware Bay in early September of 1729, there was great rejoicing.

A pilot came on board to guide the ship around the sand banks to port in the city of Philadelphia. No one was allowed to leave until a doctor checked passengers for disease. The journey had surely tested their faith and endurance. Sixty-four males, fifty-eight females and five male children under age fifteen had survived the trip.

Peter Becker and German Baptists in Pennsylvania greeted the expected new immigrants. Since Peter knew Alexander well, he embraced and kissed him. Because Alexander did not speak English, Peter helped the group sign legal papers. They also had to agree to honor the King of England who ruled this land, but they were not required to take an oath.

The new arrivals traveled to Germantown by wagon. During the seven-mile ride on the Philadelphia Road, Peter thanked Alexander for his willingness to come to America. The Mack family stayed in Becker's log home north of town. Alexander and Peter spent long hours in front of the stone fireplace discussing their plans for the future. Peter gladly gave leadership of the Germantown church over to Alexander.

Alexander met his new neighbors with enthusiasm. Mennonite and Quaker groups had settled in Germantown earlier. Their stone and framed houses faced the main street which had once been part of a swamp. Most townspeople were linen weavers by trade. Alexander toured the gristmill and the paper mill. However, after building their own house, Alexander's family also decided to make their living as weavers.

Alexander spent most of his time ministering to members of his congregation. Besides leading worship services, he visited the sick. Alexander showed genuine concern for his people just as he had done in Germany and Holland.

All the original members of the 1708 baptisms in Schwarzenau, except one, came to Pennsylvania. In America, the German Baptists renewed their belief in community and the teachings of Jesus. Besides worshiping on Sundays, they humbly honored God in their daily living.

Even in Pennsylvania, members argued about church practices. These disagreements caused Alexander great concern. The German Baptists came in contact with many more customs than they had known before.

Four years later, John Naas, the last German Baptist leader in Germany, sailed to America. During the next decade, new church groups were started west and south of Germantown. As German Baptists went out to tell others about their beliefs, their membership continued to grow.

In 1732, there was yet another problem. Some German Baptists in Pennsylvania decided to live and work in a community set apart from everyone else. This group went to live at the Ephrata Community with the persuasive leader, Johann Conrad Beissel. Beissel's followers included about half the members of his Conestoga congregation and even some close relatives of the German Baptist leaders.

Beissel had come to believe that the German Baptist Brethren, as they became known, were not spiritual enough. He thought that the return of Christ would happen in their own lifetime, and they should be prepared, day or night. While trying to understand these ideas, Alexander's health failed. In early 1735, nearing the age of fifty-six, Alexander Mack died.

At his funeral in Germantown, many friends and religious leaders gathered to show their deep respect for the humble life of Alexander Mack. They recognized the sacrifices and contributions of this intelligent man who had inspired spiritual commitment. There was a long service of preaching and hymn singing inside the Mack home. Afterwards, Alexander Mack was buried in a small field at the edge of town. Only a simple stone slab marked his grave.

In Germantown, the German Baptist Brethren continued to meet for worship with Peter Becker as their leader. They met in a large house built by Christopher Sauer and his son. Sauer invited new arrivals from Europe to his home. Later, the Germantown congregation elected both Christopher Sauer, Jr., and Alexander Mack, Jr., to the ministry.

With approval from the Germantown church, Christopher Sauer set up a printing press. He printed many projects including a newspaper, an almanac and an ABC primer. In 1742, he printed the first German-language Bible in America.

By 1770, there were fifteen German Baptist Brethren congregations in Pennsylvania and seventeen in Virginia, Maryland and the Carolinas. Until then, Brethren groups practiced the custom of worshiping in homes. But in 1770, the Germantown congregation built its first separate stone meetinghouse. Much later, in 1894, Alexander Mack's grave was relocated to the burial ground behind this first meetinghouse. In fact, six generations of Alexander Mack's descendants are now also buried there.

Today, this first meetinghouse of the German Baptists in America serves as a church and a museum. Located in Germantown, Pennsylvania, the building is also a center for community activities. Both Mack's family and succeeding generations of family groups in the German Baptist Church have thrived in their new homeland.

Since the first adult baptisms in Schwarzenau, Germany, Alexander Mack's leadership has rippled the waters outward with far-reaching influences. Among the Brethren over the years, there have been further debates on many issues. Even so, they strive to carry on the rich legacy of Christian community and spirituality exemplified by Mack's life.

Mack's followers have spread their beliefs great distances beyond one small German village. With church members in many nations, Brethren have played leading roles in peace actions, faith sharing, missions and relief work. They often partner with other denominations. As Brethren face challenges in the twenty-first century, they continue to fulfill Christ's command to share the message of peace, service and salvation throughout the world.

The Brethren Denominations

The 1708 baptisms at Schwarzenau, Germany, were the beginning of a church denomination called the Brethren. The earliest church members were known as New Baptists, and later, German Baptists and German Baptist Brethren. An Annual Meeting to discuss the beliefs and policies of the church has been held every year since 1742. In 1908, a main branch took the name, Church of the Brethren. Today, an Annual Conference gathering worships and conducts business for more than a thousand Church of the Brethren congregations throughout the United States and in more than a dozen foreign countries.

Besides the Church of the Brethren, several other branches of Brethren trace their roots to Alexander Mack's vision. Among them are the Old German Baptist Brethren (1881), the Brethren Church (1883), the Dunkard Brethren (1926), the Fellowship of Grace Brethren (1939), and Conservative Grace Brethren International (1992). These groups all work together with representation on the Brethren Encyclopedia, Inc., Board of Directors. In total, over twenty combined Brethren bodies include more than 4,000 congregations located in twenty-three nations.

Alexander Mack (1679-1735)
Timeline of Life Events

1679, July 27	Alexander Mack is baptized in Schriesheim, Germany, at the Reformed Church.
1688	Grandfather Johann George Mack dies.
1690–1691	Town appoints Mack's father as mayor.
1692	Mack is confirmed in the local Reformed Church.
1701, Jan.	Mack marries Anna Margaret Kling.
1701, Nov.	First son of Alexander and Anna Mack is born (John Valentine).
1702	Alexander's mother, Christina Mack dies.
1703	Second son of Alexander and Anna Mack is born (John).
1704	Mack meets Ernst Christoph Hochmann.
1706, June	Alexander's father, John Mack, dies.
1706, Aug.	Alexander Mack family flees to Heidelberg.
1706, Dec.	Mack family moves to Schwarzenau, Germany.
1708, Aug.	Eight persons are baptized in the Eder River at Schwarzenau and become known as New Baptists.
1709	Hochmann cuts ties with the New Baptists.
1712, Jan.	Alexander Mack, Jr., is born to Alexander and Anna Mack.
1714+1716	Two daughters are born to Alexander and Anna Mack (Christina and Anna Margaret, who dies as an infant).
1715	Mack publishes *Rights and Ordinances.*
1719	Krefeld German Baptists migrate to Germantown, Pennsylvania.
1720, May	Schwarzenau Baptists move to Friesland, Holland.
1720, Sept.	Mack's wife, Anna, and daughter, Christina , die in Holland.
1723, Dec.	Peter Becker organizes the church in Germantown, Pennsylvania.

1729	Thirty German Baptist families, led by Alexander Mack, migrate from Holland to America.
1730	Alexander Mack becomes leader of the Germantown congregation.
1732	Johann Conrad Beissel organizes the Ephrata Community.
1735, Feb. 19	Alexander Mack dies in Germantown, Pennsylvania.
1770	First church service is held in new Germantown meetinghouse.
1894	Alexander Mack's grave is moved to the cemetery behind the 1770 Germantown Church.

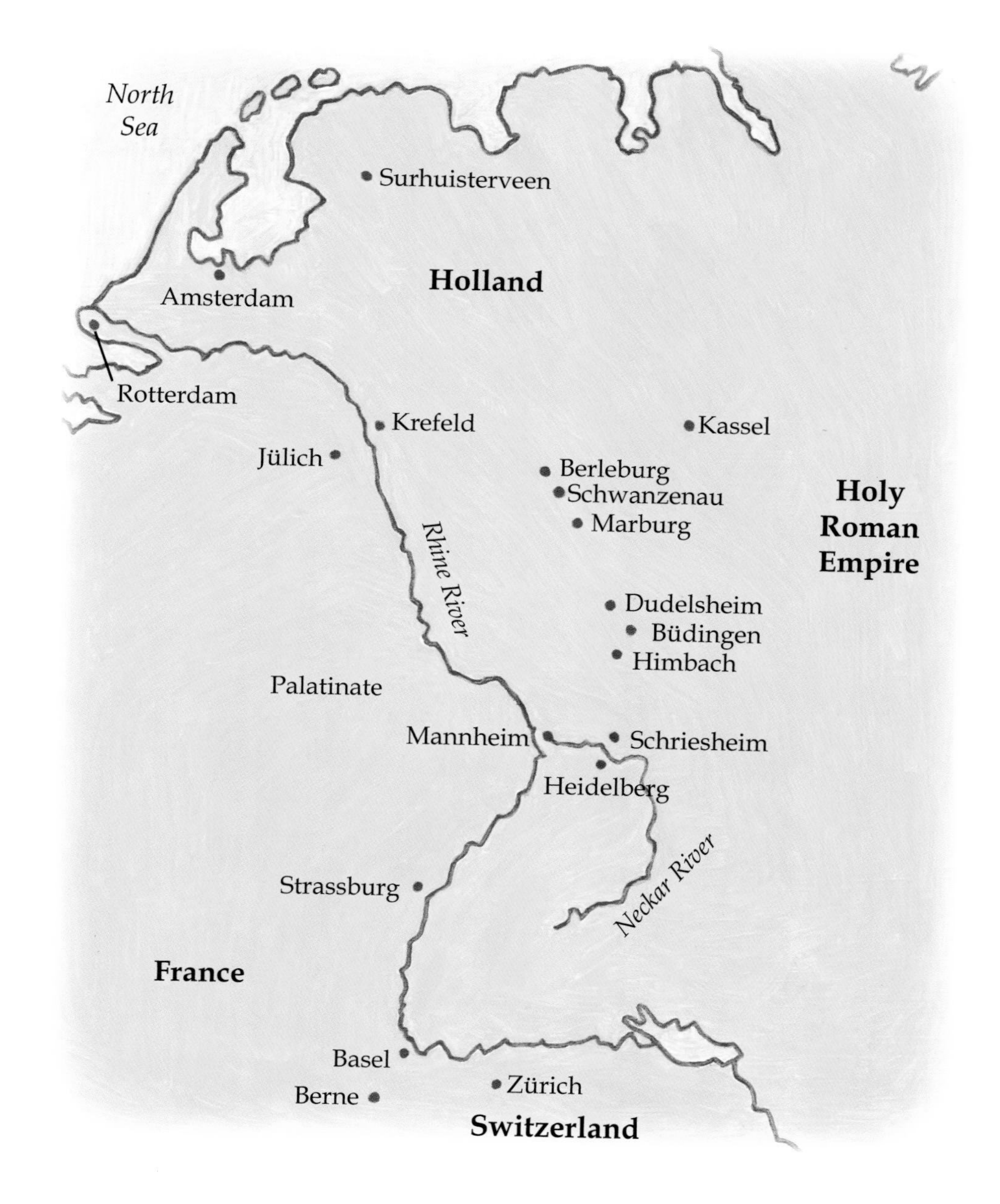

Bibliography and Sourcebooks for Adults

Bittinger, Emmert F. *Heritage and Promise*. The Brethren Press, Elgin, IL: 1983.

Bradley, John. *Ephrata Cloister, Pennsylvania Trail of History Guide*. Stackpole Books, Mechanicsburg, PA: 2000.

Durnbaugh, Donald F. *Brethren Beginnings: The Origin of the Church of the Brethren in Eighteenth-Century Europe*. Brethren Encyclopedia, Inc., Philadelphia, PA: 1992.

Durnbaugh, Donald F., editor. *The Brethren Encyclopedia, Volumes 1 and 2*. Brethren Encyclopedia, Inc., Philadelphia, PA: 1983.

Durnbaugh, Donald F. *European Origins of the Brethren*. Brethren Press, Elgin, IL: 1986.

Durnbaugh, Donald F. *Fruit of the Vine, A History of the Brethren 1708-1995*. Brethren Press, Elgin, IL: 1997.

Eberly, William. *The Complete Writings of Alexander Mack*. Brethren Encyclopedia, Inc., Pub., BMH Books, Winona Lake, IN: 1991.

Renkewitz, Heinz, and William G. Willoughby, trans. *Hochmann von Hochenau*. Brethren Encyclopedia, Inc., Philadelphia, PA: 1993.

Shultz, Lawrence W., and Medford Neher, ill. *A Mural History of the Church of the Brethren*. Board of Directors, Camp Alexander Mack, Milford, IN: 1976

Shultz, Lawrence W. *Schwarzenau Yesterday and Today, Where the Brethren Began in Europe*. Camp Alexander Mack, Milford, IN: 1954.

Stoffer, Dale R. *Background and Development of Brethren Doctrines: 1650-1987*. Brethren Encyclopedia, Inc., Philadelphia, PA: 1989.

Willoughby, William G. *The Beliefs of the Early Brethren 1706-1735*. Brethren Encyclopedia, Inc., Philadelphia, PA: 1999.

Willoughby, William G. *Counting the Cost, The Life of Alexander Mack 1679–1735*. Brethren Press, Elgin, IL: 1979.

Text Notes

Page 2 Alexander was named after his mother's brother and his godfather, Alexander Fillbrun. His uncle was a postmaster in the village of Neckarhausen.

Page 10 The color of wedding dresses worn in the time period in the Reformed Church would probably have been black (p. 11), according to Hans Joerg Schmidt, Schriesheim historian.

Page 17 Hochmann's full name was Ernst Christoph Hochmann von Hochenau, and he lived from 1670 to 1721. In the text, he is referred to simply as "Hochmann." A traveling evangelist with a magnetic personality, Hochmann strongly influenced Mack's conversion.

Page 20-21 Buildings in Schwarzenau are shown as they may have appeared in the early 1700s. These include the manor house, various homes and the Valley of Huts. A later castle in Schwarzenau was not built until 1788.

Page 25 The first baptism included five men and three women. Besides Alexander and Anna Mack, there were Andrew and Joanna Boni, George Grebe, John and Johanna Kipping and Lucas Vetter.

Page 26 Alexander Mack did not seek the role of leader, but because of his skills and finances, others looked to him for guidance. Mack is known as the inspirational leader, first minister and organizer of the German Baptists.

Page 29 Hochmann opposed all forms of church organization, and he became more vocal in his criticism of the New Baptists. There is uncertainty about whether or not Mack and Hochmann ever reconciled. Hochmann remained in Schwarzenau, and he died a year after Mack's group left for Holland.

Page 40 The ship, the Allen, was a very small passenger ship. The voyage was the first trip across the Atlantic Ocean for its British captain, Master James Craigie. The voyage usually took six or seven weeks. Mack's voyage on the Allen lasted ten weeks.

Page 49 The Ephrata Community became known as Ephrata Cloister, which described the lifestyle of its inhabitants. Some original buildings still exist in Ephrata, Pennsylvania. The site is now a National Historic Landmark administered by Pennsylvania Historical and Museum Commission. Ephrata residents made many contributions in the areas of colonial education, music, literature and art.

Besides members of the Conestoga congregation, seventeen Germantown Brethren went to live at Ephrata in 1739. Two sons of Alexander Mack, including Alexander Mack, Jr., and his brother, John Valentine Mack's family, became part of the settlement. Alexander Mack, Jr., left after ten years. Maria Sauer, wife of Christopher Sauer I, lived at Ephrata from 1731-1745.

Page 49 Sources disagree about Mack's age at death. It was the custom to baptize new babies a few days after birth. Mack was baptized July, 1679, and he died Feb. 19, 1735. Thus, he was still 55 years of age at death (according to *The Brethren Encyclopedia*).

Page 50 There are discrepancies in various sources concerning architecture of the 1770 Germantown meetinghouse before later renovations, particularly with window shapes.

About the Artist
Mary Jewell

Mary Jewell of Pennsylvania, calls herself "A Storyteller in Pictures." Mary grew up in a Church of the Brethren, near Gettysburg, along with her four brothers and four sisters. Her art education began at the Art Institute of Pittsburgh. After rearing three children, she studied at the University of Edinboro, and received a BA in Art from Shippensburg University in Pennsylvania.

Mary works in realism and uses some of her impressions from America and abroad as themes. Art, to her, is a powerful language that expresses itself across time and space. She wants her paintings to tell a story that will excite or relate to the viewer. She likes to create subjects that are Christian, cultural and nostalgic. Most of her work is created in oils, but she also does pen and inks, sculptures and watercolors as well.

Mary has had a varied career. Besides art, she has managed youth hostels and worked for the Department of Agriculture. Later, while living in Bulgaria and Albania, she combined art and teaching. In the Balkans, she painted several life-sized murals for children's orphanages and schools. More recently, she worked with troubled teens in a security unit in Pennsylvania.

Mary has had showings of her artwork in Pennsylvania, and she has displayed pieces as part of collections in several states and in Canada. Mary has a strong interest in the life of Alexander Mack because she is an eighth-generation direct descendent of Mack through her mother. For Mack's story, she traveled to places in Germany related to Mack's life and did research in historical archives while there. Mary believes that God gives gifts and talents to His creation, and she is learning to respond as a steward to this calling.

Additional artwork by Mary Jewell can be viewed on her website, www.jewellhistories.com.

Left: Westfälische Rundschau, Lars-Peter Dickel

About the Author
Myrna Grove

Myrna Grove has been a career elementary teacher in Ohio for many years. She has a Bachelor of Arts in Education from Manchester College in Indiana and a Masters degree in Library Science from Kent State University in Ohio. She grew up in the Church of the Brethren, and has attended its national Annual Conferences throughout her life.

An early acquaintance of hers was Brethren historian, L. W. Shultz, founder and manager of Camp Alexander Mack in Milford, Indiana. Myrna's mother, Florence Stombaugh Grove, served as a camp counselor at Camp Mack, and later, their family attended family camps there.

With a strong interest in history and research, Myrna's previous non-fiction books have been *Asbestos Cancer: One Man's Experience* (1995) and *Legacy of One-Room Schools* (2000). She has traced her roots to Swiss Anabaptists in the early 1500s from the canton of Zurich, having traveled to ancestral homes in both Switzerland and Germany. She is also a member of the Hans Herr Foundation in Lancaster County, Pennsylvania, another ancestral home.

For a number of years, Myrna has been associated with the Mazza Museum: International Art from Children's Picture Books, located at the University of Findlay in Ohio. Its gallery houses the world's largest collection of original artwork from children's picture books. Myrna believes that picture books are an educational tool for all ages and the illustrations greatly enhance understanding of the story.

Myrna's biography is listed in several publications, among them *Marquis Who's Who of American Women* and *Who's Who in American Education*.

Myrna's books are available on her website, www.mgrovebooks.com and by writing to Myrna Grove, P.O. Box 801, Bryan, OH 43506.

Praise for Mack Book

"I was struck anew and again by the love of Christ and the Word of God that inhabited the very core of Alexander and Anna Mack as I read this very accessible and enjoyable book. While written for children and as a biography, it allows all ages to catch the heart devotion of the dear brothers and sisters that began a movement, and it challenges us to ask the same of ourselves."

Tom Schiefer, National Moderator, The Brethren Church, and Senior Pastor, First Brethren Church, Nappanee, IN

"I enjoyed reading Myrna's book with my daughters. It gives life and personality to people my daughters knew only by name. I appreciated the way that Myrna infused the story with the ideals of the church. My daughter, Ruth (age 13), said that it was a cool way to learn about Brethren history in such an interesting way. My daughter, Anna (age 11), said that it was fun to learn about Alexander and Anna Mack and Peter Becker. These were names she knew from buildings and monuments while attending church camp at Camp Mack."

Dorothy Ritchey Moore, former Pastor, Lick Creek Church of the Brethren, Bryan, OH

"Finally, Alexander Mack's time has come. This is the first children's book about our first leader, and it is exceptionally well done. It will inspire children of all ages to join the ranks of Brethren leaders in the next 300 years."

Jeanne Jacoby Smith, Professor of Curriculum/Instruction and Rhetoric, McPherson College, McPherson, KS

"This picturesque treatise by Myrna Grove and Mary Jewell is finely honed with historical accuracy. Its lucid script is appropriate not only for youth, but for the seasoned generations. I highly recommend it to all ages."

A. Herbert Smith, Professor of Religion, McPherson College, McPherson, KS